Table of Contents

Acknowledgements — vii

Dedication — ix

Section I
Poems of Praise — 1

Section II
Poems of Love and Joy — 19

Section III
Poems of Comfort and Peace — 39

Section IV
Poems about the Faith Journey — 59

Acknowledgements

"The heavens are telling the glory of God; and the firmament proclaims His handiwork. Day to day pours forth speech and night to night declares knowledge."
Psalms 19:1-2   RSV

I would first of all like to give thanks to the Lord, the Creator of the universe and all that is in it. This book of poems would not exist if it were not for Him. In a very real sense this is God's book. He is the One who has opened my eyes to see His attributes in the world He has created. He is the One who has inspired me through my days by the beauty of His creation. He is the One who gives me life and enables me to express the joy, gratitude, comfort and strength I feel when I see His handiwork. It is my prayer that as you read these poems, your heart will be touched by the Spirit of God and you will be able to see Him ever more clearly in the beautiful world He has created. May you rejoice greatly in His amazing love for you.

I would like to thank my wonderful husband, Bill for encouraging me to publish this work. Through the years he has been my supporter, encourager, proof reader and so many other things. I thank the Lord for the life He has allowed us to share.

I would also like to thank our son Dr. Ben and his wife Deb for the prayers and the encouragement as I have undertaken this project.

I would like to thank the ladies from my Bible Study group of Mulberry Street United Methodist Church for all their kind words, encouragement, and positive feedback on the poems I have shared with them. They are a wonderful blessing and support.

I would like to thank the members of our little village church, then called Cheshire Methodist Church, for inviting me to Vacation Bible School when I was just a little girl and feeling lost and alone. The love they showed me was truly the love of Christ and I knew somehow that I wanted what they had. They literally loved me into a relationship with Jesus the Christ and I am forever grateful.

Last, but not least, I would like to thank the many people of WestBow Press who have been so helpful in enabling me to fulfill
a desire that has been in my heart for many years, that the Lord may be glorified.

May the Lord bless each one of you!

For my husband, Bill, who has always
believed in and encouraged me.
Many thanks, my beloved!

In memory of my parents, George and Doris Andrich,
who taught me even as a child to love
God's created world.

Section I

Poems of Praise

Creation Song

There is a song if we could hear it
inherent in each bird that sings.
It is a song of celebration,
a song that praises Christ the King.

There is a song as waves go crashing
on a seaside's crystal shore.
It is a song of great Thanksgiving.
May it ring forevermore!

There is a song in stars and planets
as they circle in their place.
A song that lives within each moment
sharing praise in outer space.

There is a song in trees and flowers,
colors vibrant, strong and true.
Just by being clear and brilliant
there's a song in skies so blue.

It's a song that praises Jesus,
God the Father, God the Son
God, the precious Holy Spirit.
It unites us all as one.

May this song go on forever
sung by each created thing.
For the Lord our God has granted
each of us this song to sing.

May creation rise in chorus
as we praise the Lord of love.
May the goodness and the glory
lift our hearts to God above.

God of All Creation

God of all creation,
    how worthy is Your name.
God of all creation,
    forever You're the same.
Changeless and eternal,
    yet loving us always.
You are the One and only
    to whom I give my praise.

God of light and glory,
    You gave Yourself for all.
You left Your holy dwelling.
    I've heard Your loving call.
What wonderful redemption
    was given through God's Son.
How marvelous the joy
    when Jesus' work was done.

I can't begin to tell You,
    How much I love Your name.
It fills my heart with glory
    to think of why You came.
God of all creation,
    Your life fills up my soul.
God of all creation,
    Your love has made me whole.

Revelation

Oh Lord, my God the ocean wide
    is very deep with restless tide.
Oh Lord, my Lord, the mountains high
    frame rugged peaks and wide blue sky.
The lightning's flash and thunder's roar,
    the gentle rains and birds that soar,
all things above, all things below
    are here because Your breath did blow
across the waters deep and still.
    You made the mountains and the hill.
Then You spoke creative power,
    caused the earth to bloom and flower.
Lord, You are God of all the earth
    to each creation You gave birth.
You spoke to life each living thing
    and placed in it a song to sing.
A song of praise and thanks to You
    Who made the earth and heavens too.
Oh Lord, my Lord, what can I say
    to share Your majesty today?
How can I even comprehend
    this love of Yours that has no end?
Open wide my heart and mind
    that I may seek and always find
You waiting there to show the way
    through all the moments of my day.
For You and You alone I praise.
    Reveal Yourself through all my days.

The Dawn

Blue how blue the sky appears.
        Blue and green the sea,
gently rolling white capped waves
        moving constantly.
Silver, silver lies the sand
        waiting patiently
for the rough caress of waves
        from the restless sea.
Quiet, quiet is the morn.
        Silently the sun
creeps above the ocean
        where sea and sky seem one.

Quickly, quickly come the streams
        of sparkling, dancing light
skipping over the water there.
        Oh! what a glorious sight!
Brilliant, brilliant is the path
        of light across the way.
Peaceful, peaceful is my heart
        as dawns another day.
In all the world that I behold
        I find God's majesty.
I thank you, Lord, for sights like
        these that set my spirit free.

A Thankful Heart

Give me a thankful heart, Oh Lord,
    by highest heaven and earth adored.
Give me a heart that through my days
    speaks clear and strong Your word of praise.
Give me a thankful heart that sings
    with silver laughter-colored wings.
A heart that sees in darkest night
    the glory of Your holy Light.
Give me a thankful heart that sees
    sweet blessing in a gentle breeze.
A heart that sees You everywhere
    in crowded streets or quiet prayer.
Give me a tender heart that cares,
    a heart that trusts in You and dares
to sing its song of praise on earth
    and questions not each person's worth.
Give me a heart that's pure and true,
    that starts and ends each day with You.
And, in my life, may I impart
    Your love and grace to others' hearts.

How Good It Is!

How good it is to praise the Lord
    and thank Him every day
for all the wonders of His love
    His guidance on our way!
How good it is to praise the Lord
    to bless His holy name
to know Him as our risen Lord
    Who loves us, each the same!
How good it is to praise the Lord!
    His song is sweet to hear.
It rises with such joyfulness
    and brings our Lord so near.
How good it is to praise the Lord!
    Sing out, my spirit, sing!
The Lord has given all for us
    so let the joy bells ring!

Wonderful, Lord!

How wonderful, Lord,
    in the dawn dew-pearled,
when the light greets the day
    with its wings unfurled,
and the birds fill the air
    with their "good morning" praise,
to lift eyes to You
    in the sun's golden rays!

How wonderful, Lord,
    in the freshness of morn
to see all the world
    in a new day reborn!
To hear in the beat
    of the earth rising new
all the wonder and glorious strength
    that is You!

How wonderful, Lord,
    in the heat of the day
to offer refreshment
    as we go our way
to souls that are weary and worn
    in the heat
with the water that flows
    from Your great mercy seat.

How wonderful, Lord,
    as twilight prevails
to know that rest comes
    and never will fail
to fill with Your strength
    all who follow Your way
from the rising of sun
    to the close of the day.

How wonderful, Lord,
        in the quiet and dark
To know that Your Word
        still sings sweet as a lark.
That you never sleep
        in the darkness of night
but are leading and guiding
        with Your pure, clear Light.

How wonderful, Lord,
        that in all of our days
Your light shines through all
        with life giving rays!
We thank you, dear Lord,
        for all that You are,
our Savior and Master,
        our Bright Morning Star!

Transformation

From arid soil
      a freshened stream
flows forth
      to water flowers.
From barrenness
      green grass and bush
spring forth
      in lovely bowers.
From sinful lives
      a sweet fresh breath
comes forth
      to make us new.
From barren lives
      full joy comes forth
and wonder
      is renewed.
How can this be? By God alone
      such miracles arise.
To all who call upon His name
      He hears their broken cries.
He sends His healing balm to all
      who seek His loving grace,
and blinded eyes are opened wide
      beholding Jesus' face.

Christ is Risen!

"Christ is risen," sings the morning!
      "Christ is risen," sings my soul!
Dawn through eastern sky is breaking.
      Shades of night begin to roll.
See the darkness flee the sunlight.
      See the earth bathed fresh and new.
Clarity of vision sharpened,
      washed in sunshine and the dew.
Just as clean and fresh as sunrise
      is this life that dwells within.
Bathed with God's great love, compassion,
      setting this life free from sin.
Christ is risen! Death is conquered!
      Now our life in Him can grow.
Christ is risen! God ordains it,
      clears our sight that we may know.
Know the Christ of Resurrection.
      Know the Eternal Lord of Love.
Know the answer to our questions,
      clothed with glory from above!
Christ is risen! Christ is risen!
      Sing aloud His praise all men!
Clap your hands you trees and mountains!
      Christ is Lord! Praise God! Amen!

How?

How shall I express
        the joy that fills my heart
when I view the myriad colors
        that this changing season starts?
What words can I find
        within my stunted sphere
to give proper praise
        to the wonder I see here?
To say that it is beautiful,
        and beautiful the sight,
cannot explain my stirring heart
        that longs to take its flight.
To speak of leafy brilliance
        shimmering on the trees,
and softly drifting colored ships
        amid the sparkling seas,
and to give detailed description
        of the colors interwoven
which makes a tapestry
        fit for the floor of heaven,
can never relate to anyone
        how blessed and rich I feel
on viewing this, God's handiwork,
        surrounded by His seal.

An Autumn Day

There's something about an autumn day
        when the air is clear
        and the sky is blue.
There's something about the golden sun
        and dancing leaves
        with brilliant hue.
There's something about the rich delight
        as scents of autumn
        fill the air.
There's something about the rustling woods
        with its crinkling carpet
        of beauty rare.
There's something that speaks to me of God.
        It stirs me so,
        like bells that ring!
There's something about an autumn day
        that lifts my heart
        and makes me sing!

Autumn Beauty

The world stands
        in the autumn sun
dazzling the eye
        of everyone.
As if a giant hand
        had swept
across the earth
        without a rest,
painting leaves
        in brightest hue,
gold, red, orange
        against skies of blue.
Beauty that
        the mind can't measure.
A sight one's heart
        can always treasure.

No More

I look across the wide, wide plain
    and with my eye no longer see
the outline of the mountains
    with their awesome sense of majesty.
My eye no longer can behold
    the beauty that inspired me there,
amid the mountains' towering height,
    breathing deep the thin, clear air.

No more I see the tall green spires
    lining hills and valleys deep.
No more the blossoms beautiful
    the mountain air alone can keep.
No more the snow in mid-July,
    the streams so clear and free.
They seem to laugh as they flow along
    on a shining, sparkling spree.

No more the call of a lonely bird
    as it wings through the crystal air.
No more the feeling you, too, could fly
    if you would only dare.
These sights and sounds are far away
    in terms of miles and time,
but they're only as far as a wandering thought
    for they live still in my mind.

I See You, Lord

In sunrise mist and sunset glow
    I see Your face, oh Lord.
In sighing wind and whispering leaves
    I hear You speak Your word.
In restless waves that toss about
    I see Your power and majesty.
In crystalline sand along the sea
    I look and see Your purity.
In steady constant beating waves
    I hear Your heartbeat in the earth.
In birds that sing and bubbling streams
    I hear Your laughter and Your mirth.
In twilight, sunlight, starry night,
    trees and flowers and stony brook,
in all this world that You have made
    I see you everywhere I look.

Praise Song

Not only when the day is fair
      and life is sweet and free from care.
Not only when the sun shines bright
      and even darkness has it's light.
Not only when I have a song
      within my heart the whole day long.
Not only when the wind blows soft
      and carries fragrances aloft.
But even when the day is dreary
      and life seems hard, the way seems weary.
Yes, even when no song appears
      and in my heart are streams of tears.
Yes, even then will I sing praise
      to God, Creator of my days.
And even then will I look up
      take from His hand whatever cup
He holds, for well I know His grace,
      one day I'll see Him face to face.
And when I do, oh may it be,
      He will speak these sweet words to me,
"Well done, my true and faithful one,
      who praised Me with the shining sun
and even in the darkest night
      sang songs of praise till morning's light."

Section II

Poems of Love and Joy

The Touch of Love

Sunlight splashing, slowly falling
    through the trees like gentle rain.
Color drifting, softly touching
    leaves and bark time and again.
Dripping slowly from the treetops,
    brushing earth with pools of light
Ever touching, ever moving
    toward the heart, this lovely sight.

Tenderly enfolding heartache,
    giving balm to ease the pain,
comes the sunlight's graceful dancing
    where the dark of night has lain.
Passing glimpse of heaven's glory
    here before me now appears
and I view this scene of splendor
    through a misty veil of tears.

Tears of joy and thanks and longing
    for just what I do not know.
Something stirring in my being,
    reaching upward, aching so.
"Touch me, Lord, and loose the fetters
    of this earthly lump of clay,
Till I see Thy Face more clearly
    and reflect Thy love each day."

Love

Love is very like
      a fountain flowing free.
It is an endless stream
      giving constantly.
It reaches far
      and it reaches wide
to the very heart
      where life abides.
It flows along
      with healing power
wherever it's touch
      pervades a bower.
Dried up and almost dead
      hearts lie
until love's freshening touch
      comes by.
Just as the streams
      bring life anew
to burned up fields
      where flowers once grew.
And like a stream,
      love's not confined
to a single heart
      or a single mind.
From one heart to another
      it flows
as it glides along
      its power grows.
As streams expand
      till they become the sea,
Love reaches out,
      healing you and me.

Love Flows Down

Love is like a mountain stream,
    bouncing, leaping joyfully,
singing as it dances down
    from the mountain to the town.

Love that comes from God on high
    freely flows and freely gives,
pouring out its precious grace
    upon this needy human race.

Love fills our lives with joy and peace.
    It bubbles up like mountain streams.
When this love comes pouring in
    it cleanses us from all our sin.

Oh, give God praise, all people now!
    Let waters flow and spirits sing!
Fill all the earth with songs of praise,
    pour out God's love through all your days!

The Color of Love

The color of love is a dark, dark night
    on a hillside long ago,
When the angels sang and the sky grew bright
    with heaven's radiant glow.
The color of love is the shepherds there
    who were lost in the glorious sight,
The shepherds who followed the angel's command
    through the darkness of the night.

The color of love is a tiny babe
    in a manger cold and dim.
Where the parents watched in amazement and awe
    as those shepherds bowed before Him.
The color of love came in disguise
    for who would have thought that a king
Would come in this way, humble and mild
    yet with grace that could make the heart sing.

The color of love is this baby grown
    now a strong and gentle man,
There on a cross with its shame and its pain,
    forgiving, as only God can.
The color of love is an empty tomb
    and a Life that never dies,
and He offers us all this life giving joy,
    God's marvelous surprise!

The colors of love are with us today
    in beauty and splendor and grace.
They come with each day as we worship the Lord
    and look on His beautiful face.
Please do not lose sight of this Gift, Jesus Christ,
    Who knocks on the door of your heart.
Just let Him come in and let the joy flow
    then Christmas will live in your heart.

The Sound of Love

The sound of love is a baby's cry
    as it rang through the dark of night.
It was a sound that touched the earth
    and filled it with God's Light.
The sound of love is the angels' song
    as it filled the midnight sky.
It bid the shepherds go and see
    this baby and hear His cry.
The sound of love was like waves of light
    as they raced to this stable drear.
They saw the Child, somehow heard the love
    and knelt in awe and fear.
The sound of love came so quietly
    causing the heart to sing.
Somehow they heard, with their heart and their eyes,
    this baby was really a King!

The sound of love is God's voice in the night
    as we struggle with fear or pain.
Somehow we are able to hear His love
    and He brings us peace again.
The sound of love is sometimes lost
    in the rumbling, mumbling throng.
Yet hearts who know the sound of love
    still hear its sweet, sweet song.
The sound of love is joy and peace.
    It is comfort, shelter, grace.
It comes to all who will open their eyes
    and look on the Savior's face.
As you hear once again of Jesus' birth
    on this holy Christmas Day,
may the truth of the life that He gave for all
    fill you and show you His way.

Love's Song

Always and forever there is love
      to make us sing.
Always and forever love can
      lift our heart on wings.
Always and forever,
      deep within our very soul
there is love which calls us upward
      to the highest, brightest goal.
Though at times the way seems dreary
      with more darkness than the light,
still is love within us singing,
      chasing clouds and clearing sight.
Deep and true as life itself
      is the rhythm of this song,
beating steady, flowing surely,
      sweetly singing clear and strong.
Always and forever there is love
      to make us sing.
Always and forever love can
      lift our heart on wings.

Oh, the Great Love of Jesus!

Oh, the great, great love of Jesus!
    Love that knows no bounds of time,
Love that reaches through the ages,
    touching now this heart of mine.
Wondrous love of heaven before us
    in the Christ of Galilee,
taking all our sin upon Him,
    Sinless One, upon the tree.

Oh the great, great love of Jesus!
    How can I begin to tell
all the grace and mercy shown us
    in our Lord, Immanuel.
Grace and mercy flowing freely
    like the endless moving sea.
Still His love just keeps on coming
    pure and priceless, rich and free.

Oh, the great, great love of Jesus!
    May my heart forever sing
of His everlasting kindness
    Jesus Christ, my Lord and king.
All the world needs God's pure mercy
    in these days of toil and strife.
May our lives show forth God's promise:
    sins forgiven, eternal life.

Affirmation

It seems almost too beautiful to bear,
the shining sun, the cool, rain freshened air.
The sparkling drops of rain glistening around
on trees, flowers, grass, jewels on the ground.
The rainbow in the sky of colors bright,
and just a part of sky that looks like night.
The silver edged clouds fleeing fast,
the earth bathed clean and fresh again at last.
Joy rises in my heart at sound of birds,
joy bubbling forth devoid of any words.
Sweet scented air surrounds and fills my head.
Wonder I feel that never shall be dead.
I see, feel and hear in such beauty's call
there is God who cares and loves us all.

Speaking Love

The Lord can speak to me
    with the beauty of a flower
or the sparkle of a dewdrop
    in the sun's first golden hour.
The Lord can speak to me
    in a vast expanse of blue
or in the autumn leaves
    drenched in brilliant hues.
The Lord can speak to me
    in the ever changing clouds
or in the twinkling jewels
    filling night's blue velvet shroud.
But one of the most vivid ways
    the Lord can speak to me
is in the thoughtfulness and love
    that others let me see.
So I thank the Lord for meeting you
    and in this special way
speaking through the kindness that
    you've shown me since that day.

The Dewdrop

It was just a dewdrop on the grass
      that caught and sparkled in the sun.
And yet it seemed a miracle
      within its depths had just begun.
Scarce even seen without the light
      of sun to search and try it out,
but brilliant with the prisms rare
      reflecting color within, without.
The drop itself a world complete
      with beings that cannot be seen
without the aid of microscopes.
      What is it that this world can mean?

At least that small must our whole world
      seem to Our God who loves us so.
Why should He care to send His Son
      to light our world and help us grow?
Why is it we should seem so dear
      to God, Creator of the earth?
For that He loves us all is clear
      and offers to us all new birth.
A dewdrop small, almost unseen
      and then that blinding, brilliant dart
of sun's rays magnified and spread
      to make that dewdrop stand apart.

And could it be our world so small
      when seen through God's own searching light
should shine as brilliant as the dew
      with prisms clear reflecting light?
Until somehow the universe
      will turn its gaze and look to see
a brilliant light not seen before
      that suddenly is free?
God's love cleanses from all sin
      making jewels sparkling, rare.
Those now saved by God's own Son
      are products of God's love and care.

Evening Song

Still evening, twilight falls.
        The earth begins to sleep.
A flock of geese cuts a V
        across the water deep.
The ever changing colors
        across the evening sky,
fill my mind with wonder
        as I hear the wild geese cry.
Bare branches etched in black
        yet standing strong and true.
Well defined against a sky
        of deep, dark velvet blue.

Peace, peace begins to fill
        my restless weary heart.
To keep this lovely memory
        will always be a part
of what I am and who I am.
        It was lovely from the start.

Winter's sleep is almost here,
        but other memories come
of warmer times and brilliant leaves
        glistening in the sun.
How wonderful Your earth, Oh Lord
        in all its different ways.
No matter what the season
        I shall lift my voice in praise.
You are never changing, Lord,
        my times are in Your hands.
Thank You, lovely, precious Lord.
        In Your great love I'll stand.

Flight

So high I am it scarcely seems
        I'm anywhere but in my dreams.
The sights to view high in the air
        set free my mind much as I dare.
That bank of cloud's a desert
        with softly drifting dunes.
And now above the clouds
        appears the brilliant moon.
That bank of cloud's a castle
        dark, silent in the night.
And those are steep white mountains.
        Oh, what a glorious sight!
The sun sinks long and slowly,
        a streak across the sky.
Beneath, the lights like jewels
        so bright and sparkling lie.
It is another different world
        so far above the land.
I could almost, I think, reach out
        and touch God's loving hand.

So High

Shining wings eclipsed against an azure sky.
    Soaring body, with him I seem to fly
up toward the sun away from earth and care,
    I feel the wind soft, playing with my hair.
I see new things I never dreamed I'd see.
    I feel such joy I never knew could be.
No hindrance here of pressure, rules or time,
    still higher up we both begin to climb.
I hear sweet songs from wind within the trees
    and feel the cool and gentle touch of breeze.
Yet still I feel the earth firm under me,
    the earth a lock, but in the mind a key.
And now he's gone and I remain below
    yet feel the wind still soft around me blow.
And will that wondrous moment ever return?
    That precious time for which I daily yearn?
Yes! Yes it will, for earth can never bind
    the spirit moving freely in the mind.

Delight

Oh Lord my God, I scarce can tell
    the joy I feel this day,
in thinking of Your grace and love,
    the true and living way.
This joy is deep and rich with life.
    It gives me strength complete,
and with leaves rippling in the wind,
    it gives me dancing feet.
My heart wells up with songs of praise
    as I behold Your face.
I see the brilliant blue of sky,
    Your likeness there I trace.
In flowers delicate and bold,
    with colors rich and rare,
I somehow see Your loving hand
    that placed each one with care.
Let all creation sing Your song
    of life and joy and love,
so You alone are lifted up
    and praised in heaven above.
For You alone deserve all praise
    Creator of all things.
Now my heart rises high and wide
    and with creation sings.

Simple Things

In simple things I find great joy.
        In simple things great rest.
The glint of sun on a bluebird's wing
        the babies in their nest.
The sound of the wind among the leaves
        that shimmer in the breeze.
The songs of birds throughout the day,
        the drowsy hum of bees.
The acrobatic squirrels that climb
        and swing from dizzy height.
The multicolored flowers blooming,
        what a lovely sight!
The scent of blossoms in the air,
        a note from someone dear.
The sunlight dancing on the water
        under skies so clear.
In simple things I find great joy
        for in such things I see
the hand of God who made them all,
        Who loves both you and me.

The Plane

It lumbers graceless as a bus
    while moving still upon the ground.
Its engines whine and roar so much
    you cannot hear another sound.
How slow and painful seems its pace
    as it wends its tortuous way
to the place where speed can gather
    and straight, so straight is the way.
At first it stops, then creeps again,
    then faster moves along.
The movement, speed, excitement
    almost become a song.
Momentum builds, the engines roar,
    the moment's almost here.
Then suddenly, earthbound no more,
    it cuts the sky so clear.
It leaves behind its clumsiness
    much as a fledgling swan.
A soaring, silver, graceful bird
    flying toward the dawn.
Just so shall we be one day free
    from the earth's strong gravity.
We'll soar on Spirit wings of love
    and Jesus' face we'll see.

Ever Present Lord

Lord You are here in the darkness of night.
    Lord You are here in day's brilliant sunlight.
Lord You are here in the sun and the rain.
    Lord You are here in the joy and the pain.
Lord You are here everywhere we can be,
    for You are omnipotent, boundless and free.
How I give praise to You, Almighty King.
    How my heart lifts high Your praises to sing.
Lord You are here in the silence of prayer.
    Lord You are here and You lift every care.
Lord you are here in the crowds on the street.
    Lord You are speaking Your truth clear and sweet.
Always and everywhere You may be found,
    if we just pay attention we will hear the sound
that alerts us to hear You wherever we are
    that we may be led by You, Bright Morning Star.
May we be quick to listen and quick to obey,
    for Your presence is with us, with us to stay.
May we share You freely, Lord Jesus the Word,
    until everyone in the whole world has heard
the great, glad good news that Jesus is King.
    He cleanses our sin and makes our heart sing.
To God, God alone be all glory and praise!
    May the whole earth proclaim it through all of our days!!

Wondrous Joy

Oh wondrous joy, great gift of God
      to see us through our days.
If we will seek in the darkest night,
      we will find joy's bright rays.
This joy that comes is unexplained
      by anything on earth.
It only comes from Christ himself.
      We praise God for Christ's birth.
This blessed Christ, Immanuel,
      God with us every day.
In Him is joy pure and complete
      as we give thanks and pray.
You are so wonderful, Lord God
      Who numbers all our days.
May we in all we say and do,
      show to the world Your praise.

Joy! Joy! Joy!

Long years ago, the angels sang,
    Joy! Joy! Joy!
That night the earth and heavens rang.
    Joy! Joy! Joy!
They sang of Jesus' lowly birth.
    The Son of God came down to earth,
and offered all mankind new birth.
    Joy! Joy! Joy!

That night the shepherds stood in awe.
    Joy! Joy! Joy!
As angels sang of what they saw.
    Joy, pure joy!
The Son of God has come this day
    to Bethlehem on bed of hay.
Go now to worship Him and pray.
    Joy! Joy! Joy!

The star shone brightly on that night.
    Joy! Joy! Joy!
The wise men guided by its light.
    Joy, pure joy!
Bringing precious gifts so rare
    to the infant lying there,
showing Him their faith and care.
    Joy! Joy! Joy!

And so we come to You, our Lord,
    Joy! Joy! Joy!
by highest heaven and earth adored!
    Joy, pure joy!
We come and feast our hungry eyes
    on a Child who opens paradise,
and fills our hearts and gives our lives
    Joy! Joy! Joy!

Section III

Poems of Comfort and Peace

Quiet Time

The earth stands with such clarity
    against the morning sun.
The brilliant lights of stars above
    go slowly, one by one.
The velvet blue of early morn lightens
    shade by shade.
The rays of sun creep in and through
    the forest to the glade.
The birds chirp sweetly, strong and clear,
    their notes on fluted wing.
Silent my lips, but how my heart
    joins with them as they sing.
Leaves, grass and shrubs seem emerald green
    spotlighted in the dawn.
The dewdrops glisten much as diamonds
    sprinkled on the lawn.
The gentle wind strokes, bends the leaves
    and sets them shimmering
as waves upon the ocean fly
    on silent golden wings.
An airy, lacy string of pearls waves
    softly in my sight.
All's light and life and joy and peace
    as quickly flees the night.

My Lord

As waves so gently bathe the shore
        and constantly do change the sand,
Your Presence bathes my weary soul
        and molds it with Your loving hand.

The sand waits silent, patiently
        for the touch of sea to bring it life.
My soul's great longing seeks You out
        and finds You when it's torn with strife.

The winds caress and touch my hair
        surround me gently here.
You stir within and touch my heart,
        enfold and draw me near.

Your Presence and love I hold more dear
        than jewels sparkling, rare.
I fly to You and rest secure
        within Your tender care.

Safe Harbor

The seas were rough and the waves were high,
    and it seemed that no one heard my cry.
The wind was strong and my strength was gone
    and I wondered how I could ever hold on.
Then a voice spoke out in the midst of my fear
    and said, "Be still. My child, I am here.
I am the Master of wind and sea
    and all you need do is look at Me.
Do not ponder the wind and rain
    but look away, turn your eyes again
to the One who alone can calm the sea.
    The Lord Jesus Christ, yes it is He.
Hold fast to Christ in the stormy night
    and the Lord will shed His shining light."
So to all who are fighting a raging storm
    and longing for a brighter morn.
I give these words the Lord gave me
    as a song of hope in a stormy sea.
Though the storm may rage with angry cry
    and it seems as if it will never pass by,
yet the Lord will give a safe haven of rest.
    In the midst of the storm you will truly be blessed.
For our God alone knows what is in store,
    and He's with us to keep us safe evermore.

One Lone Bird

One lone bird in a wide blue sky
      and a heart that aches as the world goes by.
"Lord of land and sea and sky,
      do You feel my pain, do you hear my cry?"
I hear the water and see the sun
      as the fresh new day has once more begun.
My heart cries out to the Lord of all
      "Please heal my heart", is my fervent call.
"Let forgiveness come from Your mercy seat
      and Your healing power in the summer heat."
One lone bird in a wide blue sky
      and the wind and waves hear its mournful cry.
It keeps its course so strong and true
      as it wends its way through the vast clear blue.
I wonder where its rest shall come
      as it flies along toward its distant home.
I feel at one with the bird and sky
      as the wind and waves hear my cry.
"Help me keep to my course so strong and true.
      Help me come to my home through the vast clear blue.
God of heaven and earth please hear my plea
      as I seek Your presence by the endless sea.
Keep my heart in Yours till time shall cease
      and I kneel in Your presence at Jesus' feet."

Lord, You are Here

In the whisper of wind,
      in the scent of the breeze,
in the colors that flame
      and the sound of the bees.
In the fresh, crisp, clean air
      and the sky's brilliant blue,
in the world all around,
      Lord, my God, I see You.

In the trees that stretch high
      as if lifted in praise,
in the songs of the birds
      as their chorus they raise.
As the rustle of leaves
      sounds so clear from on high,
I can just hear Your voice
      in the wind's gentle sigh.

Everywhere, all around, Lord,
      I know You are there.
In the face of such beauty,
      I know that You care.
I can see You and hear You,
      feel You with me now,
and my heart rests in peace
      as before You I bow.

My Treasure House

There is a hidden storehouse
        of treasure deep within.
It's always at my beck and call
        despite the world's great din.
It holds within it wondrous things,
        the beauty of God's grace,
and if I look there long enough,
        I'll see my Lord's dear face.
This storehouse does not tempt the world.
        It has no paintings rare,
nor silver, gold nor diamonds bright
        will you find buried there.
But what is there can win a soul
        that suffers in distress
and it affords a resting place
        when sorrows on me press.
This treasure house has life itself
        and gives me sweet relief
from all the things that, in this world,
        cause me to suffer grief.
This treasure house is Christ Himself
        and He my treasure rare.
He is my life and strength and joy,
        He lifts my every care.
So, often to this house I fly
        when cares begin to pain,
I see His face, I praise my Lord,
        and peace is mine again.

Just in Time

Just in time, Lord, you send the rain
    to a soul that is thirsty and parched with pain.
Just in time, Lord, the sun's golden glow
    fills all the heart so Your child can know
that You send the rain and the sun as we need
    to grow straight and strong and produce fruitful seed.
Just in time, Lord, may we know without doubt
    that deliverance will come with glad cry and shout.
Just in time, Lord, we give praise to you, King,
    and glorify You in our lives in each thing
that comes just in time to teach us Your way
    and leads us from darkness to Your glorious day!

Safe in the Arms of Love

Safe in the arms of Love,
   oh what a wondrous thing!
Safe in the arms of Love
   where my heart freely sings.
Oh, Lord, of earth and sky,
   we cannot know Your frame,
yet safe in the arms of Love,
   You gently speak our name.
How wonderful this thought
   when earthly treasures flee,
safe in the arms of Love,
   true treasures now we see.
Safe in the arms of Love,
   what wondrous grace is given.
Safe in the arms of Love
   until we reach our haven.
No storms or waves will shatter,
   clear shall our vision be,
safe in the arms of Love,
   now and eternally.

My Hiding Place

There is a place where I can go
      whenever things go wrong,
a place where all is light and peace
      and I still sing my song.
There is a place where hope is found
      and joy's my dwelling place,
where Christ my Lord communes with me
      as I look upon His face.
This place is always close at hand
      wherever I may be.
It's always open, night or day,
      there is no entrance fee.
That fee's been paid by Christ my Lord
      so many years ago.
All I need do is enter in,
      it's heaven here below.
Where is this place you ask, my friend?
      It's hidden deep within.
God welcomes me with open arms
      and casts away my sin.
My heart rejoices in the love and grace
      He freely gives
and in His Presence always near,
      my spirit truly lives.

Your Way

You know, oh Lord, the path for me
        that sets my broken spirit free.
You know, oh Lord, how I must go
        the fullness of your love to know.
Forgive the weakness of my heart
        that lets the painful teardrops start.
Forgive my fearful heart today
        and keep my feet upon Your way.
For Lord, I know that all you bring
        will lead me to my Heavenly King,
and everything that I must lose
        will be replaced by what You choose.
And Your choice, Lord, will be the best
        so in Your grace I fully rest.

Enough

Enough, oh Lord, yes let it be
    that You will be enough for me.
Beyond all things that I may own,
    may my trust be in You alone.
Within the beauty of this world
    may I see You with grace unfurled.
May I see You in everything
    that makes my spirit lift on wings.
For in You, my Lord and King
    I find the song that I must sing.
May others hear and find in You
    enough in all they say and do.
Enough, oh Lord, let it be true
    that all will find enough in You.

The More I Live

The more I live, the more I see
        of the earth's majesty,
the more I feel there must be
        Creator God behind it.
As older I begin to grow
        and my mind begins to widen,
the more I know that God is real,
        from me He's no more hidden.
The more I search and strive to find
        beauty, love around me,
the more I feel the Father's hand
        gently here surround me.
So as I stretch and try my wings
        of ever growing love,
I feel God's ever present help
        below me and above.
Ready still to bear me up
        whenever I may fall,
when others try to quell my spirit
        rising to His call.

Comfort

Although the way seems dark and drear
        I know somehow my Lord is near.
His dwelling place is deep within.
        His presence keeps me from all sin.
I do not always understand
        the way my path should go,
but that the Lord guides every step,
        somehow I always know.
He is my Light when all is dark.
        He is my strength and stay.
He is my joy when sorrow comes.
        My tears He wipes away.
Oh, how I praise this precious King,
        my Savior and my Lord!
My voice will ever lift in song
        to thank Him for His word!
His word is all my joy and peace.
        His word is all my life.
His word is dwelling in my heart
        and gives me rest from strife.

Under His Shelter

Under the shelter of God's loving hand,
      even in weakness my Lord helps me stand.
Under the cover of His love and grace
      my sin is forgiven, forever erased.
Under His mercy my heart finds release.
      In the flow of His love all my fears truly cease.
Under the guide of the Spirit of God
      I am taught day by day as I travel this sod.
Under the wonder of salvation sure,
      I feel God's great cleansing, refreshing and pure.
How can I ever stop singing His praise,
      this Almighty God, the Ancient of Days?
How can I thank Him for mercy so free
      Who has cast all my sin in the deepest sea?
All I can do is to give Him all praise,
      live in Him and love Him for all of my days.

Wilderness Walk

In the midst of bitter waters
      Lord, to You we raise our cry.
In the trials that assail us
      Lord, You will not pass us by.
In Your word that You have given
      You have promised You will be
forever near to us, and so
      we lift our voice to Thee
You have promised. You will answer
      as You did in days of yore
for Your faithfulness is constant
      as the waves upon the shore.
You have promised and will do it
      for in Christ is all we need,
and Your Holy Spirit fills us
      in thought and word and deed.
Lord, we praise You for
      this truth that You alone can give
and we praise You for Your mercy
      given us each day we live.
Sweet for bitter, full for empty,
      life for death we all receive
by Christ's death and resurrection,
      new life comes if we believe.
Thank You, Jesus for Your coming.
      Thank You, Father for Your Son.
Thank You, blessed Holy Spirit
      as You guide us one by one.
Lead us in God's truth and mercy,
      More with every passing hour,
until the day we see God reigning
      in His glory and His power.

Transforming Love

Out of the mist have I come unto Thee.
        Out of the darkness comes light.
Out of confusion comes infinite grace
        breaking the hold of the night.
Out of the pain and the sorrow of life
        quickly now comes precious joy,
out of the crucible tried by the fire,
        pure, free of any alloy.
Out of the seeking comes treasure untold.
        Out of the struggle comes rest.
Out of the worst that could possibly be,
        God brings out only the best.
Out of the doubting comes strong clear faith,
        out of the aching the balm.
Out of the cries of despair from our heart
        rings forth the loud triumph psalm.
God now transforming all that seems wrong
        bringing into sweet accord,
all that has been in confusion and loss
        by the power of His living Word.

My Prayer

May every path that my feet take
    be taken for my Savior's sake.
May every trial that I go through
    somehow reflect God's love so true.
May every dark and dreary place
    shine bright with Jesus' lovely grace.
May every joy that makes me sing
    be songs of praise to Christ my King.
May all the laughter in my heart
    reflect the love that God imparts.
And may each day that I spend here
    be filled with sweet communion dear.
This is my prayer, Oh God Most High.
    May I love You more as time goes by.

Compassionate Lord

Oh great compassion, pure and sweet
    I find each time at Jesus' feet.
Encouragement and strength to face
    the day ahead with God's great grace.
Tenderness and patience, too
    I find each time I look to You
my Savior, King, my blessed Lord,
    Who lives within my heart adored.
Praise be to You, Almighty King.
    May I ever Your praises sing.
May I stand steadfast in the fight
    and journey toward Your perfect light.
Oh Lord, my God how great You are.
    You shine as heaven's brightest star.
All praise and glory to Your Name,
    may all the world sing forth Your fame,
until the day when all shall see
    Your truth proclaimed eternally.

Section IV

Poems about the Faith Journey

My Treasure

I longed for a treasure
      of vast, untold wealth.
I longed for a treasure
      of joy, beauty, health.
I searched and I searched
      for long lonely years,
and all that I found
      was heartache and tears.

I searched and searched
      both east and west,
thinking "Here at last
      I'll find my rest."
In the north and the south
      I searched on the run,
but my treasure seemed
      as far as the sun.

Then one day I happened
      a small church to see.
I went on inside
      and on bended knee
I found the treasure
      I had searched for so long.
It was as close to me
      as a prayer and a song.

If you, too
      for a treasure long,
then don't run so far
      or so fast or so strong.
Just go to God
      on bended knee
and your treasure is there.
      Only God has the key.

A Daily Walk

In the morning's early light
    I come to seek Your face,
for well I know each day I live
    I need Your perfect grace.
I need Your presence, precious, dear
    to lead me through my day.
I need Your holiness and truth
    to shed light on my way.
Too many times my precious Lord,
    I hurry, rush and run.
I miss the chance to hear Your voice
    until the day is done.
Forgive me please for all the times
    I fail to see You there,
inviting me to stop a bit
    to show someone You care.
I need new ears to hear Your voice
    directing me each day.
I need new eyes to see the ones
    who need Your living way.
So, Lord my God, may I once more
    begin each day with You.
That I may reach the ones in need
    in all I say and do.
Oh Lord my God do dwell in me
    and shine Your purest light.
May others see You are the One
    to guide them through the night.

The Rose

As a tightly folded rosebud
      holds its fragrance deep within.
So, sometimes, we hold ourselves aloof
      from God, from friends and kin.
If the rosebud never opened,
      never saw the light of day,
it would never show its beauty
      or the fragrance of its way.
It would never show the wonder
      of the petals open wide,
drinking in the light and beauty
      giving fragrance from inside.
It would never reach fulfillment
      of what God has built within.
It would wither, fade and crumble
      if it kept itself turned in.
So it is that if we never
      open up our lives to God,
we would wither as the rosebud
      lying dead upon the sod.
We must let ourselves be yielded
      to the moving of God's hand,
that His fragrance may flow through us
      spreading goodness in the land.
We must let His Spirit move us,
      open up the petals wide.
Let His beauty shine out through us
      like an ever flowing tide.

The Fragrance of God

As a flower opens wide
    one petal at a time.
So our lives from day to day
    unfold in love sublime.
Every day we walk with God
    is new and fresh and sweet,
as we open up our hearts
    and learn at Jesus' feet.
Many years may sometimes pass
    before we understand
just how it is God works in us
    and holds us in His hand.
Yet as the time keeps passing by
    more quickly with the years,
we see the Lord in everything.
    We feel Him dry our tears.
We grow to love Him more and more
    with every passing day.
We glory in His faithfulness
    each time we kneel to pray.
So may it be that we become
    a blossom full and bright,
that gives forth color, fragrance rare
    to bless the darkest night.

My Life is Yours

Lord, my life to You I give.
      Father, daily let me live
in such a way that I may show
      the lost and weary where to go,
that they may find the comfort of
      Your great and rich redeeming love.
Father, let me light the way
      that seems so dark from day to day.
May the words I speak, in time,
      a rich and fruitful harvest find.
May all know You dwell within
      and have redeemed my life from sin.
As a star so long ago
      heralded a time of light,
may my star shine faithfully
      helping ease the darkest night.
May the life I live for Thee
      help to set Your people free.
May Your living Word of truth
      be heard throughout the whole wide earth.
All I am or yet can be
      my Father God, I owe to Thee.
And I pray my life may prove
      a vessel of Your gracious love,
that Your name may be glorified
      as I travel by Your side.
May all mankind hear Your dear voice
      and in Your gracious love rejoice.

We Never Know

We never know as we pass this way
      how our lives may speak from day to day
of our Savior's love so faithful and true
      in the little things we say and do
We never know how the things we say
      can touch other's hearts as we go our way
and lead the lost to our Savior's side
      or dry the tears that another has cried.

We never know how our acts of grace
      can reveal the love of our Savior's Face
and bring relief to a soul in pain
      and cause new hope to rise again.

So it is we must with faithful stride
      keep walking close to our Savior's side.
That the world may see in the way we live
      what wondrous joy our Savior gives,
so their hearts might warm to the Savior's touch
      and receive the healing they need so much.
May our walk with Christ be faithful and true.
      May we give God praise in all we do.

The Vine

"I am the vine" our Savior said,
      "and you the branches fair.
He who abides within my love need
      never feel despair."
The vine provides life-giving power
      long as the two are one,
but branches wither if they break
      and touch no more the Son.
Sometimes the branch is weighted down
      and parasites consume,
unless the union's strong enough,
      the branch will meet its doom.
The branch can never, on its own,
      presume to bear good fruit.
Without the vine there is no strength,
      without the vine, no root.
So if your life seems powerless,
      this union then survey.
Is there a break or parasite
      that must be done away?
Is your heart truly one with Him
      who offers rest from strife,
and is God's wondrous love and peace
      reflected in your life?

To God Alone

Lord, I have no hope but You.
        No trust but in Your heart.
So, Lord, may You in righteousness
        Your grace to me impart.
How lovely are You, Lord
        how worthy of all praise.
I would lift up my voice to You
        and sing through all my days.

Oh, Lord You are the One,
        the blessed holy Lamb,
the sacrifice for sin and shame,
        the righteous, great I AM.
To You alone I bow,
        to You my praises give.
Lord, may I never stray from You
        as long as I shall live.

May others see Your Light
        reflected day by day
in how I live my life,
        in all I do and say.
How worthy are you, Lord
        Who saved me from my sin.
You cleansed my heart.
        You gave me joy that bubbles up within.

How lovely are You, Lord,
        Your word is ever true.
And so, my Lord I give myself,
        give all I am to You.
Thanks be to You, oh Lord
        Whose heart is open wide.
Who reached this lost and lonely one
        and in my heart reside.

What can I do or say
        to thank You for this thing
that You have placed within my heart
        that causes me to sing?
It is a song of gratitude
        You planted in my soul.
It fills me up and overflows.
        Your love has made me whole.

The Jewel

Oh child of God, there is a jewel
      deep within your heart.
It is a jewel that shines so fair
      it makes the teardrops start.
It is the jewel of a yielded life,
      of trust so deep and real,
that it reflects the utmost love
      a human heart can feel.
It is a jewel, precious, fair
      that only a few can see,
but its radiance is a guiding light
      that points the soul to Me.
How true it is that I alone
      know of the victories won.
But to the victor comes the spoils
      after the battle's done.
So let your love and trust shine on,
      oh, child of God so dear.
For your fair jewel will light the way
      and banish others' fear.

Perfecting Love

Lord, I would not build You an altar of stone
    but one that is built in my heart alone.
Lord, I would not ask only blessing from Thee,
    but all that would shape and complete perfectly
the image in me that You have begun,
    the true image of You in Your own precious Son.
Lord, I do need in this time and this place
    a special reminder of your love and grace.
For all of the fears that would turn me away
    surround and harass me as day succeeds day.
But I know your Spirit is strong to uphold
    and purify me till I shine forth as gold.
So I sing praise to Your most holy name
    Who are through the ages forever the same.
Patient and loving, merciful, kind
    restoring to yours the gift of sound mind.
Thank You, dear Lord, Redeemer and King.
    Thank You, dear Lord, for each single thing
that comes to restore, recreate, to make new
    and fills with your love and grace all my life through.

The Circle of God's Will

In the center of the circle
      of the will of God I stand.
Though He leads me through the valley
      yet He always holds my hand.
He has never yet forsaken
      and has promised He will be
within my life forever,
      for He made my eyes to see.
My heart is filled with wonder
      that this Holy God of love
would choose me as a child
      and cleanse me from above.
In a close and sweet communion
      He would teach me all His ways,
that I might live with joy and gratitude
      filling up my days.
How merciful this Lord
      Who has given life to all
who have heard His voice of mercy
      and responded to his call.
All praise to You, our mighty king
      Who fills our lives with grace.
May we fill all the earth with praise
      till we see You, face to face.

River of Praise

There flows from God a wondrous stream of life.
It reaches from the very throne of heaven,
cascading through eternities of time to touch
each one of us and give us leaven.
Oh may we rise to heights unknown before
and glimpse the vision God alone has planned.
May we reach far, far beyond ourselves
and strive to reach that distant glorious land.
Each note of praise we lift to our dear Lord
is like precious dew drop in His sight.
Then as we grow in praising His dear name
the drops join in a spray that takes its flight.
It touches, blends, is drawn into that stream
of love that flows from our Creator's heart.
It floods us with His wondrous power and might
and knowledge that, in Him, we have a part
in that wide, high, free loving plan
that was in His mind when He the world began.

A Song Came

A song came to mind
      as I sat by the way
and listened to birds
      and felt the sun's ray.
A song came to me
      as I thought of my King.
As I thought of His mercy,
      my heart did sing.
My heart sang with joy
      for His marvelous grace.
As it flowed from my lips
      I almost saw His face.
As I thought of His gifts
      my heart sang its song
for His mercies and goodness
      last all the day long.
But when I thought of Him
      in His goodness and love
my praises went higher
      to heaven above.
For of all of the gifts
      He has given to me
His presence in wonder
      is what I most see.
Thank you, dear Lord
      not for things that You give,
but for just being You
      and making me live.

In the Presence of the Lord

In the presence of the Lord there is joy beyond compare.
In the presence of the Savior there is strength and hope to dare.
In the presence of the Lord there is peace and comfort near.
In the presence of the Lord there is nothing left to fear.
In the presence of the Lord there is fellowship complete.
In the presence of the Lord as I kneel at Jesus' feet.
In the presence of the Lord I can feel His love and grace.
In the presence of the Lord I can look upon His face.

In the presence of the Lord I can clearly hear His voice.
In the presence of the Lord in His heart I can rejoice.
In the presence of the Lord all the worry fades away.
In the presence of the Lord I can face another day.
In the presence of the Lord I can reach out in His love.
In the presence of the Lord I am strengthened from above.

How I praise the God of glory as I see His lovely face,
and my heart lifts up on wings as I rejoice in His embrace.
What a love our Savior offers to each one who hears His call,
and responds with great rejoicing to the One who gave His all.
In the presence of the Lord in His love so pure and true,
I can hear His word of blessing and the world is made anew.

Rest

No need to fear the drought, My child,
    for life is ever near you.
No need to fear the blazing sun,
    for my Life shadows over you.
No need to fear the barren land
    where life is never seen,
for life abides in Me, My child,
    forever lush and green.
No need to fear the desert path
    that leads through dust and sand,
for you are hid in Christ, My child,
    it is I who hold your hand.
No need to fear the vast expanse
    of seeming endless days,
for all the while I lead you, child,
    in each and every way.
So drink anew each day you live
    from water sweet and clear.
Refresh yourself within My love
    and know that I am near.
Rejoice in Me and you shall find
    a peace you never knew.
It comes to those who dwell in Me
    and find Me always true.

Amazing World

Amazing world! Those planes so high
through clouds and storms and perils fly.
The instruments so carefully built
controlled by hands with knowledge filled
can steer those planes as straight and true
as if the sky was clear and blue.
Yet should it be that either fail,
destruction sure would be its tale.
And so it is if we would fly
straight to God's heart as time goes by,
lines of communication clear
so that no static interfere
must fill our lives and spirits too.
Then God's great love can shine right through
and guide unerringly as day
our spirits as they wing their way
to destinations yet unknown,
but crystal clear when we have grown
into the Image of God's Son
whose death and life have made us one.

Pilgrimage

There is a Way that I must follow
      through the darkness of the night.
There is One who leads forever
      with a life of dazzling Light.
The way is rocky, steep and shadowed
      and the stones would overthrow,
but a gleam of light keeps drawing
      to a destiny I do not know.
There are places on the way
      that flood my being with delight,
and I would rather stay forever
      than move again into the night.
Yet somehow I know that if
      my footstep should be stayed
marvelous truth I'd somehow miss
      and so I walk on unafraid.
Sometimes darkness will surround me
      and my courage falters so,
then I think of Him I follow
      and with new faith I onward go.
Sometimes hunger will assault me
      for it seems it's been so long
since I've tasted of His Presence
      and partaken of His Song.
And a thirst burns in my throat
      for water from His Living Well
and my heart begins to question
      if I'll ever with Him dwell.
But I read His word that's with me
      and His Spirit moves again
and my heart that's parched with dryness
      fills with love that falls like rain.
There is always in my being
      that which calls me ever on
from the darkness that I dwell in
      to the glorious, bright new dawn.
I know this comes from God
      in His wondrous love and grace,
so I give my very being,

    my love, my thanks, my praise.
Though He leads me through the valley
    I cannot lay by the call
that requires the very highest
    dedication of them all.
Not content to glimpse His Presence,
    I must see Him face to face,
to reach the fullness of His stature
    through His unbounded love and grace.